DATE DUE

D1308794

DEMCO, INC. 38-2931

EXTREME ENVIRONMENTAL THREATS™

UNDER A BLACK CLOUD

Our Atmosphere Under Attack

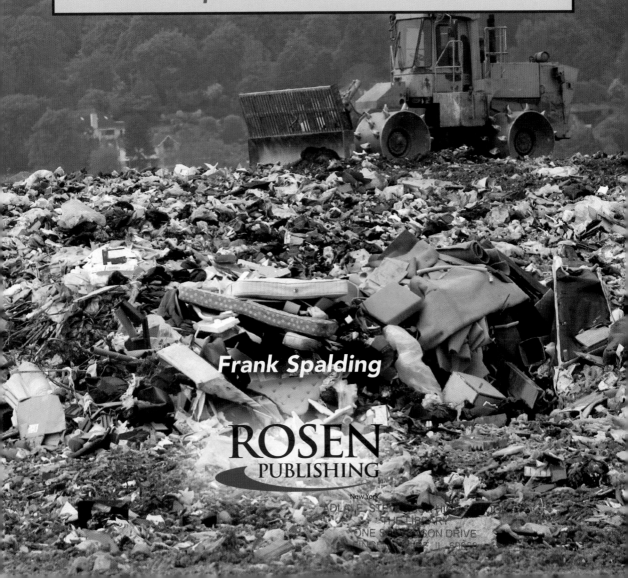

Frank Spalding

ROSEN
PUBLISHING®

New York

For Sally Ganchy—thanks for everything, Sally

Published in 2009 by The Rosen Publishing Group, Inc.
29 East 21st Street, New York, NY 10010

First Edition

Library of Congress Cataloging-in-Publication Data

Spalding, Frank.
Under a black cloud : our atmosphere under attack / Frank Spalding.—1st ed.
     p. cm.—(Extreme environmental threats)
Includes bibliographical references and index.
ISBN-13: 978-1-4358-5021-7 (library binding)
ISBN-13: 978-1-4358-5377-5 (pbk)
ISBN-13: 978-1-4358-5381-2 (6 pack)
1. Greenhouse effect, Atmospheric. 2. Greenhouse gases—Environmental
aspects. 3. Global warming. 4. Air—Pollution. I. Title.
QC912.3.S63 2009
551.5—dc22

                                                          2008019942

Manufactured in Malaysia

On the cover: A coal-burning power plant in Conesville, Ohio, spews carbon
emissions into the atmosphere, further contributing to the greenhouse
effect and global warming. **Title page:** A bulldozer shovels refuse into a
landfill, the contents of which produce large amounts of methane, one of
the more potent greenhouse gases.

Contents

	INTRODUCTION	4
1	EARTH'S ATMOSPHERE	8
2	GLOBAL WARMING	16
3	THE IMPACT OF A WARMING ATMOSPHERE	30
4	FINDING SOLUTIONS	41
	GLOSSARY	54
	FOR MORE INFORMATION	56
	FOR FURTHER READING	59
	BIBLIOGRAPHY	60
	INDEX	62

INTRODUCTION

Many major cities, like Los Angeles, suffer from heavy air pollution, including sulfur dioxide, carbon monoxide, and ground-level ozone that create smog.

No other planet in the known universe has an atmosphere like Earth's. And as far as we know, no other planet supports life. An atmosphere is a collection of gases surrounding a planet. Our atmosphere provides animals with the oxygen they breathe and plants with the carbon dioxide they need to grow. But beyond that, our atmosphere is an important buffer between the warm Earth and freezing outer space. It plays a crucial role in regulating Earth's temperature. Our atmosphere's

so-called greenhouse gases, including carbon dioxide, methane, nitrous oxide, and water vapor, trap the sun's warmth and heat Earth's surface to a temperature that can sustain life. In short, our atmosphere is what makes life on Earth possible.

Over the millennia, our planet has experienced a number of ice ages—long periods when Earth cooled and glaciers covered much of the planet's surface. Earth has also experienced warmer periods when glaciers melted and life spread toward the poles. Throughout it all, the atmosphere has always played a crucial role in keeping the planet the right temperature for life to thrive.

Recently, however, scientists have discovered strong evidence that human activity is upsetting our atmosphere's delicate balance of gases and warming the planet. Power plants, airplanes, and automobiles powered by fossil fuels emit (or release) carbon dioxide, a greenhouse gas, into our atmosphere. Factories, agriculture, deforestation, and landfills also contribute greenhouse gases to our atmosphere. These green-house gas emissions do more than just create smog and pollution. They actually trap more of the sun's heat. They are slowly raising the planet's temperature and altering its weather patterns. Global warming has already contributed to the melting of glaciers and ice caps. As our climate continues warming in the future, we can expect to see droughts, extreme weather patterns, mass animal extinctions, and rising sea levels.

In 2007, the world's foremost authority on global warming and climate change, the Intergovernmental Panel on Climate Change (IPCC), issued a report saying that the temperature of Earth's air and oceans is rising. According to the IPCC, there is over a 90 percent chance that this temperature increase cannot be solely attributed to natural processes—human beings are responsible as well. There are some scientists who remain skeptical that human beings are contributing to climate change, but they are in the minority.

Scientists are still working to understand exactly to what extent our activities damage or alter the atmosphere and to predict what our future might look like should we continue on our destructive path. Meanwhile, individuals, communities, businesses, and governments are finding ways to decrease humanity's impact on the atmosphere. Many of the world's governments are working together to reduce global carbon emissions. More and more communities are taking advantage of clean power sources, such as wind and solar power, and implementing programs such as curbside recycling and public transportation. Businesses are finding ways to become "greener," or less harmful to the environment.

A great number of new technologies are allowing individuals to be more energy efficient, and more are expected in the future. For instance, biofuels and hybrid automobile technology have risen to prominence in the last decade and may soon be widely available. Individuals can also reduce the amount of greenhouse gases they contribute to the environment in simple ways, such as saving electricity at home or buying locally grown food.

EARTH'S ATMOSPHERE

Earth's atmosphere as seen from outer space may look pristine and crystal clear, but it is under assault from greenhouse gas emissions.

To understand the threat posed to our atmosphere, we must first understand how the atmosphere works. Earth's atmosphere is a collection of gases. Earth's gravity, the same force that keeps our feet on the ground, keeps these gases from floating off into space. The atmosphere consists of approximately 78 percent nitrogen, 21 percent oxygen, and less than 1 percent water vapor, argon, carbon dioxide, neon, helium, and other gases.

The atmosphere has several layers, much like the layers of an onion. Taken together, these layers can be divided into two major sections. The first section begins at Earth's surface and ends at an altitude of approximately 60 miles (100 kilometers). It is known as the homosphere. The homosphere contains the air we breathe and is where weather occurs. The gases in this section are all mixed together and are in a constant state of motion. The second section is known as the heterosphere and consists of all the gases above an altitude of about 60 miles (100 km). The heterosphere is basically outer space. Earth's gravity exerts a weaker pull on the gases in the heterosphere, which remain separate instead of mixing as they do in the homosphere.

The homosphere contains three layers of atmosphere, as well as part of a fourth: the troposphere, the stratosphere, the mesosphere, and part of the thermosphere.

TROPOSPHERE

The atmosphere's most active layer is known as the troposphere. The troposphere encompasses all of Earth's weather and contains the clouds you see in the sky. It is also the atmosphere's largest layer, accounting for over 75 percent of Earth's atmosphere. The height of the troposphere varies. Its greatest height is about

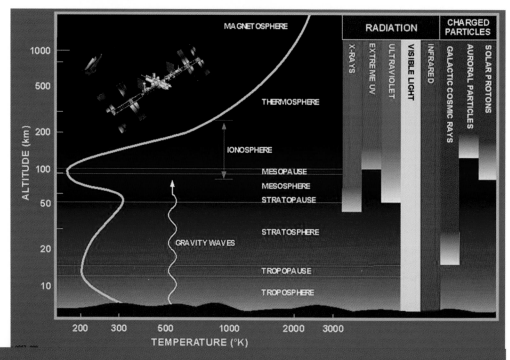

Some of the sun's light and energy is blocked by the atmosphere before it can reach Earth, while visible light and infrared radiation make it to the planet's surface. The sun's energy is measured in degrees Kelvin (273.15 degrees Kelvin is equal to 0 degrees Celsius and 32 degrees Fahrenheit).

11 miles (18 km), and its lowest is about 6 miles (10 km). The temperature of the troposphere decreases with altitude.

STRATOSPHERE

The boundary marking the end of the troposphere is called the tropopause. Beyond the tropopause lies the stratosphere, which begins at an altitude of 6–11 miles

(10–18 km) and ends at about 30 miles (50 km). The stratosphere is generally cloud free, and there is no weather. Much like the troposphere, the temperature of the stratosphere changes the higher one goes. However, unlike the troposphere, the stratosphere gets warmer, rather than colder, as altitude increases.

The stratosphere grows warmer because it contains the ozone layer. Ozone is a gas made of three oxygen atoms bonded together. It is generally created in the stratosphere when ultraviolet (UV) radiation from the sun breaks apart oxygen molecules, which are made of two oxygen atoms. The single oxygen atoms end up bonding to oxygen molecules, creating molecules with three oxygen atoms: ozone.

Ozone comprises less than 1 percent of our atmosphere, and 90 percent of Earth's ozone is concentrated in the stratosphere. The greatest amount of ozone in the stratosphere is located about 9–25 miles (15–40 km) above Earth's surface. However, ozone can be found elsewhere in the atmosphere, especially in the troposphere.

The ozone layer protects human beings and other animals from harmful solar radiation. Ozone absorbs the sun's UV radiation, which can cause burns, cancers, and even genetic damage. If you've ever gotten a sunburn, you've experienced the effects of UV radiation firsthand. Luckily, the ozone layer blocks 97–99 percent of the sun's UV light.

THE UPPER ATMOSPHERE

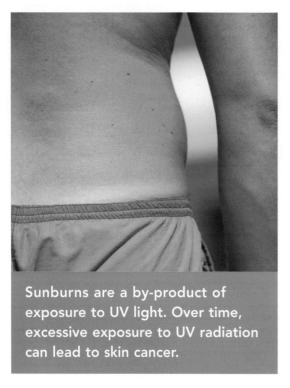

Sunburns are a by-product of exposure to UV light. Over time, excessive exposure to UV radiation can lead to skin cancer.

Past the stratopause—the upper boundary of the stratosphere—lies the mesosphere. It starts about 31 miles (50 km) from Earth's surface and ends at about 50–56 miles (80–90 km). As with the troposphere, the temperature decreases the higher one ascends. If you've ever seen a shooting star, you actually saw a meteor headed toward Earth that burned up in the mesosphere. Out of all the layers of the atmosphere, the mesosphere is the coldest.

Approximately 53 miles (85 km) from Earth's surface, the thermosphere begins. The thermosphere stretches beyond the homosphere, and most of it actually lies within the heterosphere. Just past the beginning of the thermosphere, outer space begins. This is marked by a boundary known as the Kármán line. The Kármán line is 62 miles (100 km) above Earth's surface.

The further from Earth's surface one travels, the thinner the atmosphere grows. For instance, New

The Hole in the Ozone Layer

In 1985, scientists discovered that a great deal of ozone was missing over Antarctica. It was determined that this "hole" in the ozone layer was caused by ozone-depleting gases, such as chlorofluorocarbons (CFCs), which are used as liquid coolant and in certain foams. When the hole in the ozone layer was discovered, countries all over the world acted swiftly to try to minimize, if not reverse, the damage. The 1987 Montreal Protocol was signed by 180 countries, pledging them to reduce the amount of ozone-depleting chemicals that they emitted. This international action has been successful, and it seems that the hole is beginning to shrink. It is hoped that someday it may vanish entirely.

Orleans, which is below sea level, has a denser atmosphere than Denver, which is approximately a mile above sea level. A person traveling from New Orleans to Denver has to adjust to a thinner atmosphere upon arrival. The Kármán line marks the place where Earth's atmosphere becomes outer space. It is no longer dense enough for aircraft to maneuver in. In fact, only astronauts have flown past the mesopause and into the thermosphere.

Within the heterosphere, the next atmospheric layer we encounter is the exosphere. The exosphere marks the outer edge of Earth's atmosphere. Gases are barely held by Earth's gravity in this layer. The exosphere is the

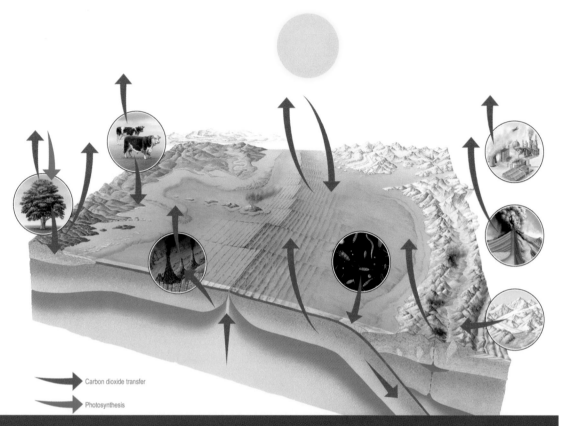

This illustration shows how carbon is exchanged between Earth's land, oceans, and atmosphere. This process, known as the carbon cycle, is being negatively affected by human activity.

outermost boundary, the furthest limit where Earth's gravity can prevent gases from escaping into the frigid void of outer space. In fact, there is no way to tell exactly where Earth's atmosphere ends: it just keeps getting thinner and thinner until it no longer exists.

A WEB OF LIFE

Ultimately, though, the atmosphere is more than just a collection of gases. It is part of a dazzlingly complex system that makes life on Earth possible. Small cycles work together to create a vast mosaic. Heat from the sun causes water from oceans, rivers, and lakes to evaporate. Evaporated water rises and condenses into clouds in the troposphere, eventually falling back to Earth as rain. Rain provides fresh water, allowing plants to grow. Plants absorb carbon dioxide from the atmosphere and transform it into oxygen. Animals, in turn, inhale oxygen and exhale carbon dioxide.

Carbon dioxide itself is just part of the greater carbon cycle, which circulates carbon through Earth's atmosphere, land, oceans, and life forms. When plants and animals die, much of the carbon in their bodies returns to Earth. Over time, their carbon can go into deep storage inside Earth's surface. Natural forest fires may release carbon dioxide into the atmosphere, which will then be reabsorbed by other plant life. The ocean has its own carbon cycles, which circulate carbon between the ocean's surface and its depths. A single significant change in the atmosphere can affect the entire system.

This woman is holding a sample of the oldest ice yet collected. It is approximately one million years old.

The idea that Earth may be warming is not a new one. It was first proposed more than 100 years ago. However, back then, scientists did not have the data to prove their theories. While measurements of the world's temperature have been recorded for a little more than 150 years, a serious examination of global warming has only begun within the last fifty years or so.

Since then, climate change scientists have learned much about how and why Earth is warming. For instance, ice masses such as those found in Antarctica contain air bubbles from hundreds of thousands of years ago. Samples of this air can be analyzed and its precise composition can be determined—allowing scientists to estimate past world temperatures. Scientists can also compare past levels of atmospheric carbon dioxide with present ones.

In 1988, the Intergovernmental Panel for Climate Change (IPCC) was established by the United Nations Environment Program (UNEP) and the World Meteorological Organization. The IPCC is composed of hundreds of scientists from all over the world. Not beholden to any single governmental or nongovernmental organization, IPCC member scientists contribute data and research and review scientific work on climate change. They do not make policy recommendations but merely provide policymakers—as well as the general public—with unbiased scientific facts.

On November 17, 2007, the IPCC released a report of its findings on global warming. According to the IPCC, the fact that global warming is happening is "unequivocal." Earth's temperature is warming, and it seems that human beings are largely to blame. How? Human beings have been altering one of the atmosphere's natural processes, known as the greenhouse effect.

THE GREENHOUSE EFFECT

Our atmosphere acts much like a greenhouse to trap some of the sun's energy and heat the planet. Imagine a greenhouse. Sunlight enters the greenhouse through its clear glass. But the glass also traps the heat of the sun inside the greenhouse. It doesn't escape to the outside world. The trapped heat raises the temperature inside the greenhouse, making it possible to grow warm-weather plants in a cold environment. Our atmosphere's greenhouse gases work in a similar way to keep Earth warm in the chill of outer space.

Venus, Mars, and Earth are the only planets in our solar system that have a greenhouse effect. On Venus, the greenhouse effect rages out of control, trapping so much heat that Venus is the hottest planet in the solar system. The greenhouse effect on Mars, on the other hand, doesn't trap enough heat, leaving the surface freezing cold. On Earth, however, the greenhouse effect traps just enough of the sun's energy to support life.

Climate scientists believe that human activity is making the greenhouse effect more pronounced. The atmosphere is beginning to absorb and retain more of the sun's energy, raising Earth's temperature. And this could prove to be a grave threat to our survival.

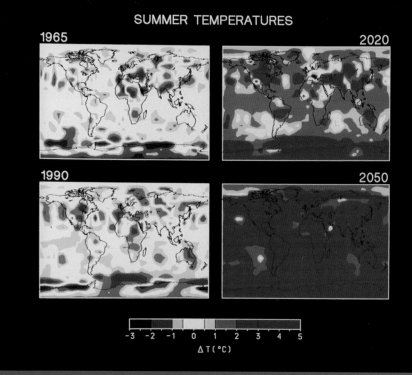

SUMMER TEMPERATURES

1965   2020

1990   2050

-3 -2 -1 0 1 2 3 4 5
Δ T (°C)

There is no question that the earth is warming. Scientists are working to predict precisely how much it will warm in the future. This NASA Global Climate Model is a projection of how Earth's climate grows hotter over time.

TRAPPING HEAT

Let's take a closer look at how the greenhouse effect works. The sun emits energy in the form of solar radiation. Some of this radiation lies within a spectrum that human beings can see as visible light. The rest exists outside of the visible spectrum as ultraviolet (UV) radiation or infrared radiation.

When energy from the sun reaches Earth, several things happen. About 70 percent of the sun's energy is absorbed by Earth's atmosphere, oceans, and land. The remaining 30 percent is reflected off clouds, snow, and ice masses back into outer space. Solar energy is reflected from Earth's surface as infrared radiation. Some of this infrared radiation escapes into space. But some is absorbed by atmospheric greenhouse gases, such as water vapor, carbon dioxide, methane, and nitrous oxide. The energy that greenhouse gases absorb warms Earth's atmosphere and surface. This "trapped" heat and energy makes life on Earth possible.

Although greenhouse gases make up only about 1 percent of the atmosphere, they have a profound effect on the temperature of our planet. Right now, Earth's average temperature is about 59° Fahrenheit (15° Celsius). If the greenhouse effect didn't exist, Earth's average temperature would be a harsh 0°F (–18°C).

The greenhouse effect isn't the only thing that can influence Earth's average temperature. For instance, changes in Earth's orbit can make the planet hotter or colder. In fact, we know that over the last 2.5 million years, Earth has undergone ice ages, when global temperatures dropped significantly. During one ice age, North America was buried under nearly 2 miles (3 km) of solid ice! Currently we are in a warming period—a warming that is at least partially caused by human activity.

Scientific evidence shows that humans have altered the composition of the atmosphere by increasing the amount of greenhouse gases it contains. In the troposphere, carbon dioxide levels have increased by about 30 percent since the nineteenth century, and they continue to increase at a rate of about 4 percent a year. Scientists believe that greenhouse gases, in turn, have caused—and will continue to cause—a phenomenon known as global warming. So far, it's impossible to pinpoint exactly how much humans are heating up the globe. However, there's no doubt that the more greenhouse gases humankind releases into the atmosphere, the warmer our world gets.

GREENHOUSE GASES

In the nineteenth century, the Industrial Revolution changed the Western world forever. By the beginning of the twenty-first century, much of the world—especially Europe and North America—had been utterly transformed. Where horses once drew buggies down dirt roads, now cars and trucks speed down asphalt highways. Once, rural families grew their own food on family farms. Today, much of our food is grown on huge industrial farms, hundreds or even thousands of miles away from our homes and shipped to our supermarkets. Once, disease, malnutrition, and squalid living conditions

Large populations put a greater strain on natural resources and inevitably create more pollution.

cut many lives short. Today, breakthroughs in agriculture, medicine, and public hygiene help people to live longer and raise more children who survive into adulthood and old age. Global populations have exploded. People have flocked to cities, causing urban populations to boom.

However, this progress comes with a steep price: the pollution that our industrialized lifestyles release into the environment. Many factories and power plants are powered by fossil fuels, such as coal and oil. When these fuels are burned, they release the greenhouse gas carbon dioxide into the atmosphere. Large-scale agriculture emits the greenhouse gas methane. So do the landfills where our trash is often sent. And as the world's population grows, the problem worsens. More people create more pollution.

CARBON DIOXIDE

One of the most important greenhouse gases is carbon dioxide, or CO_2. Carbon dioxide consists of two oxygen atoms combined with one carbon atom. Carbon dioxide is an important part of life on Earth. Plants absorb carbon dioxide and release oxygen. Animals breathe in oxygen and breathe out carbon dioxide. This exchange between plants and animals is just part of a larger process—the carbon cycle—which circulates carbon through the atmosphere to the oceans and the land.

Carbon is one of the most common elements on Earth. It is often referred to as the "building block of life" because it is the basis of every living organism. Much of the world's carbon is stored beneath Earth's surface in so-called fossil fuels, such as coal, natural gas, and all petroleum products. These fuels are the fossilized remains of ancient plants and animals. For instance, many scientists believe that oil is the remains of ancient zooplankton and algae. For millions of years, these organisms sank to the bottom of the ocean, where they were covered in more and more layers of sediment. As they sank underground, Earth's pressure and heat eventually concentrated the carbon in their bodies into oil.

Fossil fuels such as coal, oil, and natural gas provide about 90 percent of the world's energy. When fossil fuels

Coal-burning power plants, which provide the United States with a large percentage of its energy, release a lot of pollution into the atmosphere.

are burned, they release the carbon they store into the air in the form of carbon dioxide. When coal is burned in a power plant or gas is burned in a car, CO_2 is emitted into the atmosphere. This alters the balance of the carbon cycle.

The carbon cycle is dynamic, and changes to it involve so many variables that it is difficult to fully understand. Evidence shows that about half of human-emitted carbon is naturally absorbed by the carbon cycle before it can accumulate in the atmosphere. Still, scientists fear that we are radically altering the carbon cycle by burning carbon that had previously been stored deep in the planet as fossil fuels. We may be releasing so much carbon into the atmosphere that it cannot be properly reabsorbed. And when carbon lingers in the atmosphere rather than being reabsorbed by the planet and its oceans, Earth warms.

Deforestation

Earth's forests play a pivotal role in the carbon cycle. Forests absorb carbon dioxide from the atmosphere and release oxygen. Along with oceans and grasslands, our forests are "carbon sinks." They help offset, or lessen, the roughly 8 billion metric tons of carbon that human beings release into the atmosphere every year. Of those 8 billion tons, only 3.2 billion tons remain in the atmosphere to trap heat. The rest gets absorbed by carbon sinks.

Six-and-a-half billion tons of the carbon we put into the atmosphere comes from the burning of fossil fuels. The remaining 1.5 billion tons comes from deforestation. Across the world, forests are cleared every day to provide raw materials for construction, fuel for cooking and heating, and new agricultural land to feed growing human populations. Trees release carbon when burned or during the process of decaying. But that's not all. Deforestation damages the planet's ability to process carbon dioxide. Fewer trees absorb less of the carbon dioxide in our atmosphere. When forests are burned, the atmosphere gains carbon dioxide—and Earth loses some ability to absorb it.

Many scientists believe that today's atmospheric carbon levels are the highest they've been for millions of years. By taking core samples of Antarctic ice masses, which contain bubbles of ancient air that have been trapped for thousands of years, scientists can measure the amount of carbon that was contained in the atmosphere in past centuries and millennia. We know that prior to industrialization, the level of carbon in Earth's atmosphere remained fairly stable for a very long time. But after industrialization, the amount of carbon dioxide in our air began rapidly to grow. For instance, 300 years ago, before the Industrial Revolution, atmospheric carbon levels were about 280 parts per million. But in 2005, carbon levels in the atmosphere were about 380 parts per million.

METHANE

Another important greenhouse gas is methane. There is much less methane than carbon dioxide in our atmosphere, but methane is a far more potent greenhouse gas. Much of the methane in our atmosphere is produced naturally. Approximately three-quarters of natural methane emissions originate from wetlands. The rest can be traced to soil deposits of methane, emissions from termites and other animals, and emissions from the ocean.

However, more than half of all methane emissions today come from human activity. The production and refinement of natural gas and other fossil fuels, raising livestock, coal mining, municipal wastewater treatment, and even large-scale rice farming all result in significant methane emissions. The largest human-based contributors to atmospheric methane are landfills, which

Large landfills, like this one in the United Kingdom, release greenhouse gases as organic garbage decays. Recycling and composting can reduce the amount of garbage that gets sent to landfills.

release methane gas as the organic matter in the trash decays.

NITROUS OXIDE

The greenhouse gas nitrous oxide is emitted from a great number of sources. The most common human-related sources include the management of agricultural soil (such as the use of nitrogen to fertilize crops), emissions from burning fossil fuels, animal manure from human-grown livestock, and human sewage processing.

HIGH GLOBAL WARMING POTENTIAL GASES

High global warming potential (GWP) gases are so named for their significant contributions to global warming relative to their small concentrations in our atmosphere. These gases include chlorofluorocarbons (CFCs) and hydrochlorofluorocarbons (HCFCs). A third kind of high-GWB gas are halons. Once emitted, they can stay in the atmosphere for decades, accumulating year after year.

High-GWP gases are used in manufacturing and the production and processing of metals such as aluminum and magnesium. When it was discovered that high-GWP gases like CFCs caused an extreme amount of damage to the ozone layer, a concerted and largely successful effort was made to phase many of these harmful gases out of use.

OZONE

Ozone's presence in the atmosphere can be both helpful and harmful. In the stratosphere, ozone blocks harmful UV rays. But in the troposphere, ozone is a pollutant (resulting in smog) and a greenhouse gas.

Tropospheric ozone is naturally occurring but is also produced by vehicles in the form of gasoline emissions, as well as through industrial processes. As a greenhouse gas, ozone works to trap heat in the troposphere. However, ozone does not stay at such a low elevation for very long. Therefore, its true contribution to global warming is difficult to assess.

THE PRICE

As the amount of greenhouse gases in the atmosphere increases, Earth's average temperature has slowly begun to rise. For instance, Earth's temperature rose by about 1.1°F (0.6°C) during the twentieth century. By the end of the twenty-first century, surface temperatures might increase by as much as 3.2–7.2°F (1.8–4°C). That might not sound like a lot, but such an increase will have a profound effect on the environment.

THE IMPACT OF A WARMING ATMOSPHERE

The Antarctic Larsen B ice shelf collapsed in 2002. Antarctic ice has been melting at an extremely rapid pace.

Fifty years ago, when climate science was still in its relative infancy, there were about 3 billion people on Earth. Today, Earth has a population of approximately 6.5 billion people. Earth's expanding population has meant bigger cities, bigger suburbs, more cars on the road, more fossil fuels being burned to generate power, more industry, and more deforestation as trees are cut down to make way for new communities or vast tracts of agricultural land. Larger populations use up more resources: they require more food, more water, more land, and more building materials for homes, businesses, and schools. Inevitably, this all results in the emission of more greenhouse gases.

Earth has heated and cooled several times during human history. But today, for the first time in history, we are able to measure how changes in the climate impact the entire globe—from glaciers to oceans, from rain forests to deserts, from wetlands to tundras. And we are able to see how our actions have a real impact on our atmosphere.

According to the IPCC, of the years between 1995 and 2006, eleven were among the twelve warmest years since scientists began recording global temperature measurements in 1850. These high temperatures have had wide-ranging impacts on our planet. Here are a few.

MELTING ICE

Earth is home to a lot of large ice masses. From the massive ice sheets at the poles and Greenland, to permafrost in the Arctic, to icebergs floating in our seas, the planet Earth is full of ice. Large areas of ice help cool the planet, reflect sunlight back into space, and also serve as large reservoirs of freshwater. But as the ice melts, it reflects less sunlight. This sunlight is instead absorbed by the ocean, warming its waters. The warmer the ocean gets, the more the ice melts, and so on. This is known as a feedback effect: warming leads to more warming, creating a cycle that perpetuates itself.

The size of Earth's ice masses fluctuates throughout the year. They melt some in the summer and refreeze in the winter. However, as global temperatures have slowly risen, scientists have observed that less and less ice forms every year. For instance, the Arctic sea ice that returns every year is vanishing at a rate of 9 percent annually. The loss of ice at the Arctic ice cap has been dramatic. In 2005, scientists discovered that approximately 500,000 square miles (1.3 million square km) of Arctic sea ice has vanished since 1978 (the year that satellite records of the ice cap began). Since then, ice has been disappearing at an alarming rate. It is estimated that Arctic ice is at its lowest level for the last 100 years. In fact, only about half of the ice that existed in 1978 is still there. Scientists fear that if ice loss continues at its present rate, there will be no Arctic ice cap at all during the summer by 2030.

Antarctica, the huge continental landmass at the South Pole, has also lost a great deal of the ice that permanently covers it. Currently, Antarctica loses about 25 billion metric tons of ice annually. Recently, large chunks of ice have broken free from the main Antarctic ice mass. Alone and floating in the ocean, these ice chunks melt much faster.

Unpredictable Weather

One of the more unpredictable results of global warming will be its effect on our weather. Scientists believe that Earth's weather, which is sensitive to temperature changes, will become more extreme and changeable as the planet becomes warmer. This could potentially lead to millions if not billions of dollars in storm damages. Extreme weather incidents like 2005's Hurricane Katrina may become more common. During that monster storm, Katrina's surging rainwaters overwhelmed the levees in New Orleans, Louisiana, resulting in devastating and deadly flooding that killed more than 2,000 people and displaced about a million residents.

Other land-based ice masses are suffering as well. The world's glaciers, which provide an important source of fresh drinking water for many people, are shrinking. For instance, glaciers located in the Alps mountain range in Europe have shrunk by 10–20 percent over the past twenty years. The country of Greenland is all but covered with a massive, but melting, ice sheet, which scientists believe could eventually disappear. The world's permafrost, another source of permanent ice, is also beginning to thaw. Permafrost is a term used to describe land that is continually frozen. Among other things, permafrost contains deposits of methane, which are released when it thaws, contributing more greenhouse gas to the atmosphere. In northern communities built on regions of permafrost, a thaw could be disastrous. Without the stability of permafrost, buildings and roads could begin to sink.

RISING SEAS

As the ice melts, it will begin to raise sea levels. Warming oceans will also contribute to the rising sea levels. When the ocean heats up, its water expands, and sea levels rise.

Since 1993, the oceans have been rising at a rate of about 0.094–0.15 inches (2.4–3.8 millimeters) per year. Scientists believe that, by 2100, Earth's oceans could rise from about 8.5 inches (22 centimeters) to as much as nearly 3 feet (91 cm). Should Greenland's ice sheet completely melt, the water it would release into the oceans could raise sea levels up to 23 feet (7 m).

Rising oceans pose a real threat to coastal communities. For instance, cities like New Orleans, Louisiana, and Amsterdam, the Netherlands, are actually below sea level and are particularly vulnerable to flooding. The island borough of Manhattan in New York City, home to about 1.5 million people, is only 10 feet (3 meters) above sea level. And over half of the world's twenty largest cities are actually located at sea level, putting them at risk of being swamped by rising seas.

Much of New York City is only slightly above sea level. Cities like New York might be endangered by rising seas.

ACIDIFICATION

The ocean absorbs much of the carbon dioxide we emit. In fact, it absorbs about 25.4 million metric tons of carbon every day. But when the ocean absorbs too much carbon dioxide, it becomes acidic. Acidic water threatens many species of marine life. According to the IPCC, it's possible that, should the acidification of the ocean continue, the majority of marine life could die out by 2100. Some studies predict that the ocean could become 100–150 percent more acidic by then.

Other pollutants emitted into the atmosphere, such as sulfur dioxide, ammonia, and nitrogen oxides, also contribute to water acidification. These pollutants are produced by power plants and through agricultural processes, such as farming and raising livestock. When they are released into the atmosphere, they become nitric acid and sulfuric acid. When these acid pollutants return from the atmosphere to Earth, they tend to collect in coastal waters, acidifying them.

One effect of excess nitrogen in the water is that it promotes the growth of algae. When algae dies and decomposes, it uses up the water's oxygen. In areas of the ocean where this has happened, there may no longer be enough oxygen to support marine life.

FRESHWATER

Global warming will exacerbate (worsen) droughts and water shortages. Glaciers are important sources of freshwater, and communities dependent on them will be left dry. Without clean water, dehydration and hygiene become major issues. Droughts can also mean crop failures and wild fires. Places that already have few natural water resources, such as central Africa and the southwestern United States, may be particularly affected.

While the world's population is growing, its supply of freshwater is shrinking. In 2008, approximately 20 percent of people on Earth had limited access to safe drinking water. Less than 3 percent of Earth's water is freshwater, and 66 percent of that is locked away in ice masses where it is unavailable for human use. The majority of available freshwater is used for agricultural purposes. Access to clean and safe drinking water is already a major problem and will only become worse as global warming increases.

In drought-plagued Kenya, animals that have died of thirst litter the ground, while a young girl brings water back to her family.

DISEASE

Atmospheric pollution also has a detrimental effect on the air we breathe. For instance, tropospheric ozone levels are so high that in many American cities, there are days when people with breathing ailments, such as asthma, are warned to stay inside. Carbon dioxide also

This Kentucky teenager must undergo treatment for asthma. She lives in a part of Louisville with a great deal of air pollution, which is responsible for her respiratory problems.

promotes the growth of pollen-producing plants, which is bad news for people with allergies.

Global warming is expected to increase the incidence of insect-borne diseases. For instance, the disease malaria, which can be fatal if not treated properly, is transmitted through mosquito bites. As Earth warms, mosquitoes, as well as other disease-carrying insect populations, are expected to spread to areas that were previously too cold to support them. Other diseases, such as cholera, are expected to thrive in warmer weather.

The stratospheric ozone layer blocks most harmful UV radiation from reaching Earth. When pollutants such as CFCs deplete the ozone layer, more UV radiation is allowed to reach Earth's surface. UV radiation's negative health effects include eye damage, premature skin aging, skin cancer, and even genetic damage.

ANIMALS

Pollution, rising temperatures, and changing weather patterns have begun affecting animals across the globe. Ocean acidification can have deadly consequences for marine life. And as the climate's average temperatures rise, so do the average temperatures of Earth's water. Warming oceans have begun causing coral reefs to die off. The algae that live in the reef and produce food for coral and the marine life supported by coral reefs can't live in the warmer water.

Freshwater-dwelling animals are not exempt from the effects of pollution. Amphibians, such as frogs, seem to be particularly vulnerable. Amphibians are very sensitive to changes in their environment, and changes in water acidity and temperature can kill them. For instance, an organism known as the chytrid fungus, fatal to many kinds of frogs, thrives in warmer weather. Global warming has allowed it to spread to new areas. In fact, it is now believed that in South and Central America, global warming has already contributed to the extinction of many species of amphibians. And amphibian populations are dying off all over the world.

The disappearance of Arctic ice caps threatens the life of polar bears and certain types of seals. In fact, it's possible that two-thirds of the world's polar bears could be dead within the next sixty years. Polar bears are

Polar bears depend on sea ice—without it, they would drown. The fact that sea ice is beginning to vanish may result in the extinction of these creatures.

dependent on Arctic ice while hunting. If there is not enough ice for bears to hunt properly, they could starve. At the very least, they might not be able to retain enough body mass to properly reproduce. Recently, scientists have found what they believe to be among the first documented cases of polar bears actually drowning because there were no longer any ice sheets for them to cling to.

A 2007 traffic jam paralyzes the roadways in Beijing, China. Each of these hundreds of cars is spewing carbon monoxide—a greenhouse gas—into the atmosphere.

Greenhouse gases and pollutants released into the atmosphere by humans have harmed the planet. The question is, what can we do about it? The world's population is growing every day. The 6.3 billion people in the world today could grow to a staggering population of 9 billion by 2050. China and India, countries with a combined population of nearly 2.5 billion people (about 40 percent of the world's total population), are rapidly industrializing. As these countries expand their cities and suburbs, use more electricity, and buy more cars, the amount of greenhouse gases they contribute to the environment will skyrocket.

Despite the overwhelming scientific consensus that climate change is happening and human beings are contributing to it, the international community has not reached a consensus about how to address the challenges of global warming. Very few steps have been taken to reduce humanity's greenhouse gas emissions.

Still, solutions do exist. Around the world, nations, communities, businesses, and individuals are looking for ways to help fight global warming.

INTERNATIONAL TREATIES

Global warming is a problem that affects the entire world. Recognizing this, the international community has drafted a piece of legislation that aims to reduce and regulate emissions worldwide. It is known as the Kyoto Protocol. It was adopted in 1997 in Kyoto, Japan, and went into force in 2005. The Kyoto Protocol, signed by the majority of the world's nations, commits them to reducing their greenhouse gas emissions.

The goals of the Kyoto Protocol are relatively modest: nations that signed are required to cut their emissions in order to bring their combined greenhouse gas output to a level 5 percent below that of 1990. However, in order to reduce its greenhouse gas emissions, each nation must adopt changes that will affect its entire economy. New policies, such as placing new regulations on industry or increasing public transportation, must be put in place in order to cut emissions. Not every nation is willing to make these types of changes. Most significantly, the United States has not signed the Kyoto Protocol, which would have mandated a 7 percent reduction in U.S. greenhouse gas emissions.

Many people supported the idea of the United States signing the Kyoto Treaty and were outraged when President George W. Bush refused to do so.

The Kyoto Protocol was a significant advancement in the safeguarding of the atmosphere and environment. However, many believe that Kyoto is only the first step. It will take a much more significant global commitment to curtailing greenhouse gas emissions if we are to have any hope of minimizing climate change and its negative effects. Kyoto is a good start, but there is much more to be done.

ALTERNATIVE POWER

Currently, the United States derives about 50 percent of its energy from coal-burning power plants and just under 20 percent from natural gas. These power sources (especially coal) emit a great deal of greenhouse gas. In fact, the United States is the world's largest greenhouse gas producer.

About 20 percent of U.S. power comes from nuclear power plants, which emit no greenhouse gas. However, nuclear power plants produce highly dangerous radioactive waste that takes thousands of years to decay. It is therefore very important that nuclear waste is stored safely over a very long period of time. Many people are worried about the safety of nuclear power plants. Prior nuclear incidents, such as the 1986 melt-down of the Chernobyl nuclear power plant in Pripyat, Ukraine (then part of the former Soviet Union), have shown how dangerous nuclear accidents can be. Some countries are more eager to build nuclear power plants than others. For instance, nearly 80 percent of France's energy is generated by nuclear power. Because nuclear materials can be used to make weapons of mass destruction, they are closely monitored by the United Nations. The United Nations International Atomic Energy Agency (IAEA) only allows a certain number of countries to have nuclear power, meaning that nuclear energy may be an impractical long-term alternative to fossil fuels.

One major problem with fossil fuels is that they are finite and nonrenewable. Coal and oil take millions of years to form under Earth's surface. If we keep using fossil fuels at our current rate, it is possible that we could use up all of the fossil fuels that Earth has to offer. However, there are clean energies that harness Earth's abundant and renewable natural resources—like water, wind, and sun. These energy sources are renewable: they will never run out. They also pollute far less and emit far fewer greenhouse gases into the atmosphere than does energy created by burning fossil fuels.

Hydroelectric power—electricity created using waterpower—is one such clean energy source. It currently provides the United States with about 7 percent of its electricity. Hydropower produces no emissions whatsoever. Its main problem is that it affects river ecology and disturbs animal habitats. Totally renewable clean power sources, such as solar and wind power, are in use in many countries around the world. In the United States, for instance, some states get between 10 and 20 percent of their energy from wind power. These technologies currently provide only a small amount of power worldwide, but many hope that they will eventually provide much more.

Wind power is a totally clean form of energy that many people hope may eventually replace "dirty" forms of energy, such as coal and petroleum power.

Another relatively clean energy source is biomass—organic matter that would otherwise be composted in landfills. Biomass isn't a fossil fuel, but it can be burned to produce energy. It currently provides the United States with about 0.5 percent of its energy. Biomass produces carbon dioxide when burned, but it is carbon that the biomass had recently absorbed from the atmosphere. So while biomass might not be a completely clean fuel, it does not release carbon that had long been stored beneath Earth's surface, like fossil fuels do.

EFFICIENCY

While many countries would like to use greener power sources, the decision to do so is ultimately bound up in a complicated series of political and economic factors.

Growing Plankton

One technological solution to global warming that scientists explored was fertilizing the ocean with iron. They hoped that, by adding iron to the ocean, it would stimulate the growth of plankton. In turn, the plankton would absorb carbon. When the plankton died, scientists hoped it would sink, along with the carbon it had absorbed, to the bottom of the ocean, removing it from the carbon cycle. But this solution was not as simple in practice as it was on paper. First of all, an extremely large amount of iron was required to stimulate plankton growth. Additionally, the stored carbon dioxide is released if the iron supply is cut off, necessitating a constant input of iron. There are also fears that a large amount of iron added to the ocean could have unforeseen ecological effects.

For instance, the United States has large coal reserves. Because coal is an abundant natural resource in the United States, it will probably remain the country's dominant power source for some time to come. However, increasing efficiency of our existing power plants is a simple way to reduce carbon emissions.

According to the U.S. Department of Energy, work is under way to reduce emissions from coal-fired power plants. Right now, U.S. power plants are able to extract only one-third of the potential energy contained in coal. That means when coal is burned, two-thirds of its energy is wasted. If coal plants could extract the full energy potential of coal, they could theoretically release the same amount of power with only one-third the amount of emissions.

TAKING RESPONSIBILITY

National governments aren't the only entities that can work to reduce global warming. Local communities can institute recycling programs, increase public transportation, and encourage bicycle usage by creating bike lanes. Businesses can utilize efficient lighting and other green technologies and encourage employees to carpool or take public transportation to work. Individuals also bear their share of responsibility, and each of us can do things that will make a difference.

Every time that we drive a car, turn on a light, buy a product, or take a shower, we are directly or indirectly contributing carbon dioxide to the atmosphere. The amount of carbon dioxide that you contribute to the atmosphere is called your carbon footprint. There are many ways that you can make simple changes to your lifestyle in order to shrink your carbon footprint.

Transportation is responsible for much of the carbon dioxide emitted by individuals. In the United States, emissions from transportation comprise 40 percent of the country's global warming emissions. Automobiles, airplanes, motorcycles, motorboats, and many other vehicles are powered by gasoline, a fossil fuel. When gasoline is burned in an engine, carbon dioxide is released into the atmosphere. Over time, one person's carbon dioxide emissions can add up. You can reduce your carbon footprint by driving less, utilizing public transportation, riding a bike, or walking. Many families are now driving hybrid automobiles, powered by a combination of

California's Bay Bridge, which links Oakland and San Francisco, is often crowded with commuters. Carpooling can help reduce the number of cars on the road.

gasoline and electricity. These hybrids emit much less carbon dioxide into the atmosphere than conventional cars.

It's easy to understand how driving a car can contribute to global warming. But not many people realize that using electricity can also contribute to the problem. Most American power plants create electricity by burning fossil fuels. So when you save electricity, you're also reducing the amount of carbon dioxide you emit. There are many ways to save electricity at home. Efficient lightbulbs called compact fluorescent lamps, or CFLs, are more efficient than regular lightbulbs and last far longer. Better windows, appliances, and insulation can help conserve energy. Even small changes, such as moving your thermostat up two degrees in summer and down two degrees in winter, can make a big difference.

It also takes energy to deliver water to our homes and to process our wastewater before it is returned to nature. Therefore, when you conserve water, you are also conserving energy. Consider taking shorter showers, checking your toilet and faucets for leaks, or switching your garden to native plants that require less water than conventional lawns.

But don't stop there. Many people don't realize that it takes a lot of energy to produce the food that we eat, the clothes that we wear, and the other products that we buy. The factories that make these things consume lots of energy. And after the products are made, they must be transported to consumers. Sometimes, food and other consumer items may travel halfway around the world before they reach your home. That journey is probably powered by fossil fuels. So buying locally grown food and locally made or secondhand clothes can help reduce your carbon footprint.

You can also reduce your carbon footprint by buying products that use less packaging. Many products come

Recycling can go a long way towards reducing the amount of natural resources we consume and also help limit the size of landfills. These workers at a Maryland recycling plant sort postconsumer plastics.

wrapped in unnecessary layers of plastic, paper, and cardboard. It takes energy to manufacture all that packaging. When you reduce the amount of packaging you consume, you reduce your carbon footprint.

Trash disposal is another activity that creates lots of greenhouse gases. Some of our trash is incinerated, or burned. This contributes carbon dioxide to the environment. Other trash is sent to landfills. As the organic trash in landfills decomposes, it releases methane, a greenhouse gas even more potent than carbon dioxide.

So reducing your waste helps reduce the amount of greenhouse gases that you contribute to the environment.

Recycling helps reduce the amount of greenhouse gases that you contribute to the environment in two ways. First, it takes products out of the waste cycle. Aluminum cans can be recycled into more cans, rather than being sent to a landfill. Second, it helps reduce the amount of raw materials that are required to create more products. Recycling aluminum cans helps reduce the need for more aluminum production.

The perils facing our planet may seem enormous. But one person's actions can truly make a difference—and two, three, four, or fifty people can inspire even more change, as a ripple effect is created. The future of our planet may rest with you, and your actions may help determine the kind of world you and your own children and grandchildren will inherit and inhabit.

ADAPTATION

There is much we can do to try and reduce the severity of climate change. However, we cannot entirely prevent it. Humans will keep on emitting greenhouse gases, and Earth will keep warming. The question is not whether Earth will warm, but how much. And a few degrees may make all the difference in the world.

Meanwhile, scientists and entrepreneurs continue searching for new technologies that could help wean humanity from its dependence on fossil fuels. The search can sometimes seem discouraging. The technology that seems poised to rescue our atmosphere today may prove to be disastrous to the environment tomorrow. Some think that new technologies such as hydrogen fuel cells may contain the key to clean transportation, free of fossil fuels. Others hope that ethanol will prove an effective substitute for gasoline. The details of these plans may sometimes prove problematic, however. Hydrogen fuel cells require the use of fossil fuels during the manufacturing process. Ethanol takes lots of land and labor to produce and is ultimately blended with gasoline. So while ethanol may reduce carbon emissions, it is not a comprehensive solution.

However, the enthusiasm and passion that has gone into these and other "green" plans are humanity's greatest resource. We must and will develop alternate fuel sources. Perhaps one day these flawed technologies will be seen as milestones on the road to a cleaner, greener future.

GLOSSARY

agriculture The practice of raising crops or animals.

algae A species of very small aquatic plants. Algae play an important role in absorbing carbon dioxide from the atmosphere.

altitude The elevation of an object or place above the ground.

amphibian A cold-blooded animal that can live both on land and in the water.

atom The smallest particle of an element. Atoms can combine with other atoms to form substances. For instance, water consists of two hydrogen atoms and one oxygen atom.

coral Found in the ocean, coral is made from small creatures called polyps and inhabited by algae. Coral provides food for a variety of fish and other aquatic animals.

drought An extended dry period during which water is scarce.

emission The discharge of some kind of matter, usually into the air. For instance, an automobile emits exhaust.

ice age One of the periods in Earth's past during which Earth's temperature was very low and ice was widespread. The most recent ice age ended just over ten thousand years ago.

millennium A period of time that is equal to one thousand years.

petroleum A fossil fuel that is refined to make products such as gasoline.

radiation Energy emitted from an object as waves or particles.

scientist A person whose profession is the systematic investigation and determination of facts through controlled tests.

tundra An area where the ground is permanently frozen.

unbiased Without prejudice; not taking sides or having a predetermined agenda.

zooplankton Very tiny living aquatic organisms. Plankton are vegetation, whereas zooplankton are minute animals.

FOR MORE INFORMATION

Greenpeace
702 H Street NW
Washington, DC 20001
(202) 462-1177
Web site: http://www.greenpeace.org/usa
Greenpeace is a worldwide nongovernmental organization
   that has existed since 1971. Greenpeace actively
   campaigns on a number of environmental issues.

National Oceanic and Atmospheric Administration (NOAA)
1401 Constitution Avenue NW, Room 6217
Washington, DC 20230
(202) 482-6090
Web site: http://www.noaa.gov
NOAA is a part of the U.S. Department of Commerce.
   It works to improve people's understanding of the
   environment and how it can be effectively preserved.

The Sierra Club
National Headquarters
85 Second Street, 2nd Floor
San Francisco, CA 94105
(415) 977-5500
Web site: http://www.sierraclub.org

The Sierra Club is the oldest environmental organization
in the United States, having existed since 1892. It is
concerned primarily with conservation.

Union of Concerned Scientists
2 Brattle Square
Cambridge, MA 02238-9105
(617) 547-5552
Web site: http://www.ucsusa.org
The Union of Concerned Scientists investigates issues
such as climate change with the aim of creating
greater awareness among the public, governments,
and businesses.

United Nations Headquarters
First Avenue at 46th Street
New York, NY 10017
Web site: http://www.un.org
The UN is an international organization consisting of
representatives from the majority of world govern-
ments. The UN is devoted to using diplomacy to
handle international matters.

U.S. Environmental Protection Agency (EPA)
Ariel Rios Building
1200 Pennsylvania Avenue NW

Washington, DC 20460
(800) 438-2474
Web site: http://www.epa.gov
The U.S. Environmental Protection Agency is a
   governmental agency devoted to protecting the
   environment. Since 1970, the EPA has helped shape
   U.S. environmental policy.

WEB SITES

Due to the changing nature of Internet links, Rosen
Publishing has developed an online list of Web sites
related to the subject of this book. This site is updated
regularly. Please use this link to access this list:

http://www.rosenlinks.com/eet/ubc

FOR FURTHER READING

Brezina, Corona. *Climate Change*. New York, NY: Rosen Publishing, 2007.

Crump, Marty L. *Amphibians, Reptiles, and Their Conservation*. North Haven, CT: Linnet Books, 2002.

David, Laurie, and Cambria Gordon. *The Down-to-Earth Guide to Global Warming*. New York, NY: Orchard Books, 2007.

Dinwiddie, Robert, and Louise Thomas. *Ocean: The World's Last Wilderness Revealed*. New York, NY: DK Publishing, 2006.

Fridell, Ron. *Global Warming*. New York, NY: Franklin Watts, 2002.

Friend, Robyn, and Judith Love Cohen, with David A. Katz. *A Clean Sky: The Global Warming Story*. Marina del Rey, CA: Cascade Pass, Inc., 2007.

Gore, Al. *An Inconvenient Truth: The Crisis of Global Warming*. New York, NY: Penguin, 2006.

Sivertsen, Linda, and Tosh Sivertsen. *Generation Green: The Ultimate Teen Guide to Living an Eco-Friendly Life*. New York, NY: Simon Pulse, 2008.

Tanaka, Shelley. *Climate Change*. Toronto, ON, Canada: Groundwood Books, 2006.

BIBLIOGRAPHY

Appenzeller, Tim. "The Case of the Missing Carbon." National Geographic, February 2004. Retrieved January 2008 (http://science.nationalgeographic.com/ science/environment/global-warming/missing-carbon. html?nav=FEATURES).

Associated Press. "UN: Glaciers Shrinking at Record Rate." CNN.com, March 16, 2008. Retrieved March 2008 (http://edition.cnn.com/2008/WORLD/ weather/03/16/un.climate.ap/index.html).

Carlton, Jim. "Is Global Warming Killing the Polar Bears?" Wall Street Journal Online, December 14, 2005. Retrieved January 2008 (http://online.wsj.com/ public/article_print/SB113452435089621905- vnekw47PQGtDyf3iv5XEN71_o5I_20061214.html).

Eccleston, Paul. "Time Atlas Shows Effect of Global Warming." Telegraph.co.uk, March 9, 2007. Retrieved January 2008 (http://www.telegraph.co.uk/Earth/ main.jhtml?xml=/Earth/2007/09/03/eaatlas103.xml).

Eilperin, Juliet. "Warming Tied to Extinction of Frog Species." Washington Post, January 12, 2006. Retrieved January 2008 (http://www.washingtonpost. com/wp-dyn/content/article/2006/01/11/ AR2006011102121.html).

Gertner, Jon. "The Future Is Drying Up." New York Times Magazine, October 21, 2007. Retrieved

January 2008 (http://www.nytimes.com/2007/10/21/ magazine/21water-t.html?_r=1&oref=slogin).

Gorman, Christine. "How It Affects Your Health." *Time*, March 26, 2006. Retrieved January 2008 (http:// www.time.com/time/magazine/article/0,9171, 1177002,00.html).

IPCC. *Climate Change 2007: Synthesis Report. Contribution of Working Groups I, II and III to the Fourth Assessment Report of the Intergovernmental Panel on Climate Change* [Core Writing Team, Pachauri, R. K., and A. Reisinger (eds.)]. Geneva, Switzerland: IPCC, 2007.

Maslin, Mark. *Global Warming*. New York, NY: Oxford University Press, 2004.

NASA. "Recent Warming of Arctic May Affect Worldwide Climate." October 23, 2003. Retrieved January 2008 (http://www.nasa.gov/centers/goddard/news/ topstory/2003/1023esuice.html).

Poff, N. Leroy, Mark M. Brinson, and John W. Day Jr. "Aquatic Ecosystems and Global Climate Change." The Pew Center on Global Climate Change, January 2002. Retrieved January 2008 (http://www. pewclimate.org/docUploads/aquatic.pdf).

Revkin, Andrew C. "Arctic Melt Unnerves the Experts." *New York Times*, October 2, 2007. Retrieved January 2008 (http://www.nytimes.com/2007/10/02/science/ Earth/02arct.html?_r=2&oref=slogin&oref=slogin).

INDEX

A

acidification, 35–36, 39
algae, 23, 39
aluminum, 28, 52
animal extinctions, 6
Antarctica, 13, 17, 25, 32

B

biofuels, 7
biomass, 46

C

carbon
    cycles, 15, 23–25
    dioxide, 5–6, 8, 15, 20, 21,
        23–26, 37–38, 46, 48–49
    emissions, 7, 48, 53
    footprint, 48, 50–51
    sinks, 25
Chernobyl, 44
chlorofluorocarbons (CFCs), 13, 28, 38
chytrid fungus, 39
coal, 23, 26, 44, 45, 47–48
compact fluorescent lamps (CFLs), 50

D

deforestation, 6, 25, 30

E

Earth's atmosphere
    and agriculture, 21–22, 26–28,
        36–37
    and disease, 21–22, 37–38
    and global warming, 6–7, 16–29,
        33, 37–38
    how it works, 8–15
    and marine life, 23, 35–36, 39
    and polar bears, 39–40
    role of, 4–6
    and sea levels, 6, 13, 34
    and world population, 22, 30–31,
        36–37, 41–42
ethanol, 53
exosphere, 13–14

F

feedback effect, 31–32
fossil fuels, 22, 23–24, 28, 30, 45–46,
    49, 53
freshwater, 31, 36–37, 39

G

glaciers, 5, 31, 33, 36
global warming,
    explained, 6–7, 16–29, 33,
        37–38
    solutions to, 7, 41–53
global warming potential (GWP), 28
greenhouse effect, 17–20
greenhouse gases, 5–7, 20–21, 26,
    27, 28, 29, 31, 33–34, 41–42, 51

H

halons, 28
heterosphere, 9, 12, 13
homosphere, 9, 12
Hurricane Katrina, 33

hybrid automobiles, 7
hydrochlorofluorocarbons (HCFCs), 28
hydroelectric power, 45
hydrogen fuel cells, 53

I

ice ages, 5, 20
ice caps, 6, 32, 39
Industrial Revolution, 21, 26
infrared radiation, 19–20
Intergovernmental Panel on Climate
        Change (IPCC), 6, 17, 31, 35

K

Kármán line, 12–13
Kyoto Protocol, 42–43

M

magnesium, 28
malaria, 38
mesopause, 13
mesosphere, 9, 12
methane, 5, 20, 22, 26–27, 33, 51
Montreal Protocol, 13

N

natural gas, 23, 26, 44
nitrous oxide, 5, 20, 27–28, 36
nuclear power, 44–45

O

oil, 23, 45
ozone, 11, 13, 28–29, 37–38

P

permafrost, 31, 33–34
petroleum, 23
plankton, growing, 47

R

reservoirs, 31

S

smog, 6, 28
solar power, 7, 45
stratosphere, 9, 10–11, 12, 28, 38

T

thermosphere, 9, 12
troposphere, 9–10, 11, 13, 21, 28,
        29, 37

U

ultraviolet (UV) radiation, 11, 19,
        28, 38
United Nations Environment
        Program (UNEP), 17
United Nations International Atomic
        Energy Agency (IAEA), 44
U.S. Department of Energy, 47

W

water vapor, 5, 8, 20
weapons of mass destruction, 44
weather, unpredictability of, 33
wind power, 7, 45
World Meteorological
        Organization, 17

ABOUT THE AUTHOR

Frank Spalding has written several books for Rosen Publishing relating to the environment, alternative energy sources, green living, and public policy. Spalding lives in New York, where he is a conscientious user of public transportation.

PHOTO CREDITS

Cover Peter Essick/Aurora/Getty Images; pp. 1, 27 © www.istockphoto.com/Ralph125; pp. 4–5 © www.istockphoto.com/Daniel Stein; pp. 8, 10 NASA; p. 12 Peter Cade/Iconica/Getty Images; p. 14 © Gary Hincks/Photo Researchers, Inc.; p. 16 Koichi Kamoshida/Getty Images; p. 19 NASA/Science Source/Photo Researchers, Inc.; p. 22 © www.istockphoto.com/Gary Blakeley; p. 24 © www.istockphoto.com/acilo; p. 30 © www.istockphoto.com/Armin Rose; p. 35 © Stan Honda/AFP/Getty Images; p. 37 Mike Goldwater/Christian Aid/Getty Images; pp. 38, 49 © AP Images; p. 40 © www.istockphoto.com/Erlend Kvalsvik; p. 41 Cancan Chu/Getty Images; p. 43 Brendan Smialowski/AFP/Getty Images; p. 46 © www.istockphoto.com/Grant Dougall; p. 51 Tim Sloan/AFP/Getty Images.

Designer: Tom Forget; Photo Researcher: Amy Feinberg